D1481208

SKILLED TRADE CAREERS
WELDERS

by Gary Sprott

Rourke
Educational Media

A Division of
Carson
Dellosa
Education®

Before Reading: *Building Background Knowledge and Vocabulary*

Building background knowledge can help children process new information and build upon what they already know. Before reading a book, it is important to tap into what children already know about the topic. This will help them develop their vocabulary and increase their reading comprehension.

Questions and Activities to Build Background Knowledge:

1. Look at the front cover of the book and read the title. What do you think this book will be about?
2. What do you already know about this topic?
3. Take a book walk and skim the pages. Look at the table of contents, photographs, captions, and bold words. Did these text features give you any information or predictions about what you will read in this book?

Vocabulary: *Vocabulary Is Key to Reading Comprehension*

Use the following directions to prompt a conversation about each word.

- Read the vocabulary words.
- What comes to mind when you see each word?
- What do you think each word means?

Vocabulary Words:
- blueprints
- fuses
- infrared rays
- iron
- manufacturing
- vocational

During Reading: *Reading for Meaning and Understanding*

To achieve deep comprehension of a book, children are encouraged to use close reading strategies. During reading, it is important to have children stop and make connections. These connections result in deeper analysis and understanding of a book.

 Close Reading a Text

During reading, have children stop and talk about the following:

- Any confusing parts
- Any unknown words
- Text to text, text to self, text to world connections
- The main idea in each chapter or heading

Encourage children to use context clues to determine the meaning of any unknown words. These strategies will help children learn to analyze the text more thoroughly as they read.

When you are finished reading this book, turn to the next-to-last page for **After Reading Questions** and an **Activity**.

TABLE OF CONTENTS

ON THE JOB

Lasers, torches, and robots, oh my! Welcome to the wonderful world of welding. If you're a whiz at piecing together puzzles and love working with your hands, this fascinating career will get you fired up.

Welders Are a Hot Property!

The United States has 425,000 welders. That's a lot. But, it's not nearly enough for all the welding work that needs to get done. About 400,000 more welders may be needed in just a few years!

A welder's work must stand up to the toughest conditions.

Welders use special torches and equipment that create heat. The heat **fuses** pieces of metal to make a super-strong connection, or bond.

Welding makes it possible to build towering skyscrapers, mighty ships that cross oceans, and bridges and pipelines that stretch for miles.

fuses (FYOO-zez): melts two pieces of something, such as metal or plastic, together by heating them

People first used fire to shape metal thousands of years ago. Ancient warriors in the Middle East fought with swords created by hammering hot **iron** into sharp blades. This was known as forge welding because a forge, or furnace, supplied the heat.

iron (EYE-urn): a strong, hard metal that is magnetic and used to make a variety of things

A Wonderful Weld!

Welding grew popular in the early 20th century. Shipbuilding and other industries needed to connect massive steel sheets. Welding began to replace the use of rivets, or bolts, in steelwork.

Many welders work in the automobile industry, making and repairing cars.

Welders work in many industries, including **manufacturing** and construction. They make and repair parts for cars, ships, aircraft, power plants, and oil drilling. Welders are needed to rebuild old bridges and highways.

manufacturing (man-yuh-FAK-chur-ing): the activity or industry of making something on a large scale using special equipment or machinery

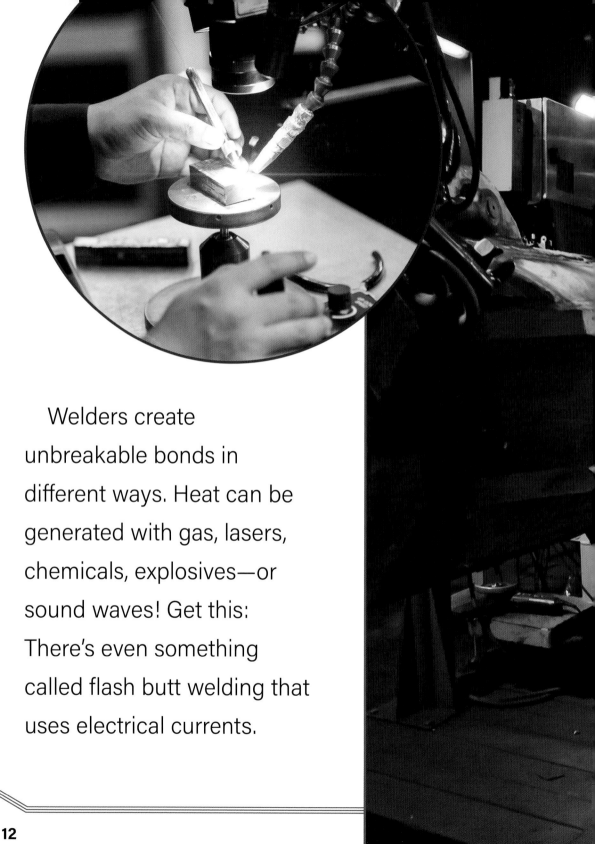

Welders create unbreakable bonds in different ways. Heat can be generated with gas, lasers, chemicals, explosives—or sound waves! Get this: There's even something called flash butt welding that uses electrical currents.

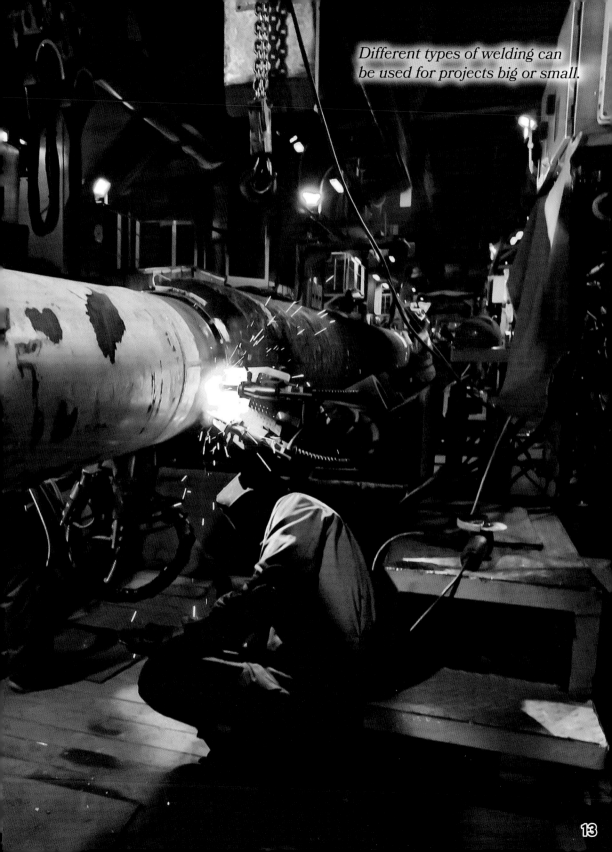

Different types of welding can be used for projects big or small.

WHAT'S IN MY TOOLBOX?

A welder's tools range from a simple hammer to a high-tech robotic laser. Powerful clamps and magnetic squares grip metal in place during welding. Temperature indicator sticks that look like marker pens show if a welded surface is hot enough. Digital monitors measure oxygen levels for a safe working environment.

New technology is giving welders many more tools of the trade.

Protective clothing keeps welders safe from head to toe.

Welders don't play with fire! They protect themselves from sparks and flames with heavy-duty aprons, gloves, boots, leggings, and jackets. Welders also work behind special curtains and screens, and even inside tents, to keep others safe from harm.

Keep an Eye Out!

Welders must shield their eyes from the blinding light of torches and lasers. The lens on their headgear darkens automatically when dangerous **infrared rays** are detected.

infrared rays (in-fruh-RED rayz): beams of radiation, or light, with long wavelengths that are outside the visible spectrum; humans cannot see them, but they can damage the eyes

Technology is changing the way that welders work. Robotic welding machines look like the arm of one of the *Transformers*. These laser welders use beams of intense light to melt metal. They are programmed to do many jobs without stopping. Robots can be used in places that would be unsafe for human welders.

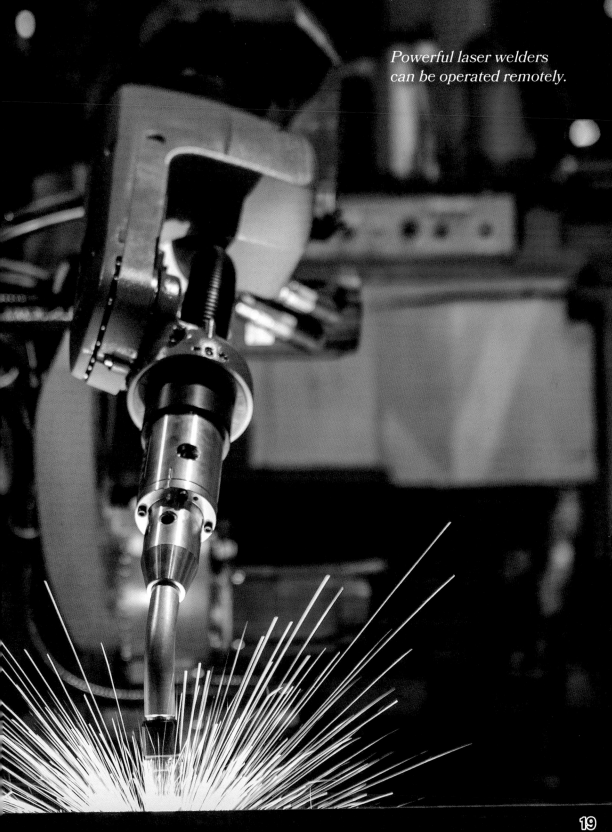

Powerful laser welders
can be operated remotely.

LEARNING THE TRADE

Has welding sparked your interest? Great! Then it's time to stay in school and study hard.

Welders need at least a high school diploma. Math, chemistry, and physics are important subjects to know well. Learning CAD (computer-aided design) will help you understand **blueprints** and other plans.

blueprints (BLOO-prints): detailed plans or models of something that will be built or manufactured

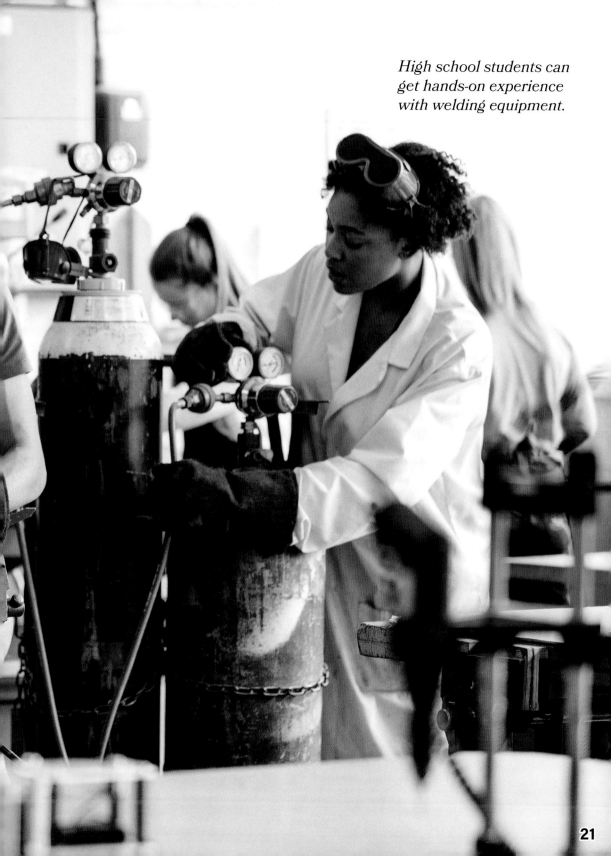

High school students can get hands-on experience with welding equipment.

Women welders helped build warships during the 1940s.

Only about five out of every 100 welders in the U.S. are women. The American Welding Society, Women Who Weld, and other organizations want to attract more women to this growing career. The groups offer scholarships, summer camps, and training workshops.

Blazing a Trail!

When men went off to fight in World War II, women took up their jobs back home. Many became welders! They built the ships and machinery that helped win the war.

Welders are important for the military. The U.S. Army's welding school includes classroom instruction and hands-on experience in the field. Soldiers learn how to create and repair metal parts for weapons, vehicles, and equipment. You could say welders keep armies *steeled* for battle!

Welding When Wet

Think fire and water don't mix? Think again! Underwater welders brave the seas to repair dams, pipelines, oil rigs, and ships. They can use air-tight cabins to work below the surface.

Welders wear diving suits and breathing equipment when working underwater.

College students learn about the science and technology of welding.

After they finish high school, many welders learn their trade at a **vocational** college. There, students discover how metals react to heat and how they can be combined. This science is known as metallurgy. They study electricity, computers, and robotics. Welding safety is also taught.

vocational (voh-KAY-shuh-nuhl): relating to a job, profession, or occupation

Apprentices are trained on-the-job by experienced welders. Like learning to play a sport or a musical instrument, practice makes perfect!

Welders can continue their education throughout their careers. Some jobs need special training and certification, such as using robotics.

United Welders

The Iron Workers Union and American Welding Society offer testing and certification for welders. Union members are in demand for high-paying jobs.

Young welders work with skilled professionals during apprenticeship programs.

MEMORY GAME

Look at the pictures. What do you remember reading on the pages where each image appeared?

INDEX

AFTER READING QUESTIONS

1. How many welders are there in the U.S.?
2. Why did welding grow popular in the early 20th century?
3. Name five things welders use to generate heat.
4. Why did women become welders during World War II?
5. What is metallurgy?

ACTIVITY

Now that you know what welders do, can you spot a weld? Find five things you and your family use that were made with welding. Do you ride a bike? How about the furniture around your house? Next, visit your local library or go online to research what types of welding might be used to create these five things.

ABOUT THE AUTHOR

Gary Sprott is a writer in Tampa, Florida. He has written books about ancient cultures, plants, animals, and automobiles. Gary's neighbor is a welder. He created a beautiful sculpture of a fish that hangs from a tree in his yard. Its metallic scales shimmer as it swings with the breeze.

www.rourkeeducationalmedia.com

PHOTO CREDITS: page 1: ©xresch / Pixabay; page 1: ©pagadesign / iStock; page 3: ©freeman98589 / iStock; page 4: ©oyen / iStock; page 5: ©GomezDavid / iStock; page 6: ©Berkut_34 / iStock; page 9: ©MarinaVarnava / iStock; page 10: ©EXTREME-PHOTOGRAPHER / iStock; page 12: ©Aumm graphixphoto / Shutterstock; page 13: ©Leonid Eremeychuk / iStock; page 14: ©mediaphotos / iStock; page 15: ©sergeyryzhov / iStock; page 16: ©South_agency / iStock; page 19: ©Thossaphol / iStock; page 21: ©SolStock / iStock; page 22: ©Ras67 / Wikimedia; page 25: ©U.S. Navy / Wikimedia; page 26: ©kali9 / iStock; page 28: ©tap10 / iStock; page 28: ©Ikonoklast_Fotografie / iStock

Edited by: Madison Capitano
Cover design by: Rhea Magaro-Wallace
Interior design by: Book Buddy Media

Library of Congress PCN Data

Welders / Gary Sprott
(Skilled Trade Careers)
    ISBN 978-1-73163-835-9 (hard cover)
    ISBN 978-1-73163-912-7- (soft cover)
    ISBN 978-1-73163-989-9 (e-Book)
    ISBN 978-1-73164-066-6 (e-Pub)
Library of Congress Control Number: 2020930169

Rourke Educational Media
Printed in the United States of America
01-1942011937